NOT YOUR USUAL UPSC BOOK

Why, What and How of the CIVIL SERVICES EXAM

NOT YOUR USUAL UPSC BOOK

Why, What and How of the CIVIL SERVICES EXAM

ADITYA BAJPAI, IRS

PRABHAT PAPERBACKS

Published by
PRABHAT PAPERBACKS
An imprint of Prabhat Prakashan Pvt. Ltd.
4/19 Asaf Ali Road,
New Delhi-110002 (INDIA)
e-mail: prabhatbooks@gmail.com

ISBN 978-93-5521-208-5
NOT YOUR USUAL UPSC BOOK
by Aditya Bajpai, IRS

Edition
First, 2022

Price
₹ 195 (Rupees One Hundred Ninety Five Only)

Printed at
Nakshatra Art, Delhi

Dedicated To:

To my parents without their blessings,
I could not be in the position to write this book.
To my wife, who has been my constant
companion in life's journey and
a solace in all the turbulence.

Author's Note

I am a 2016 batch officer of the Indian Revenue Service (Customs and Indirect Taxes). I am currently posted as Deputy Commissioner of Customs Bengaluru Customs Zone. I had held the charges of Assistant Commissioner of Bijapur division, in Karnataka and later Assistant Commissioner of Anti-Evasion in Bengaluru.

I cleared the 2015 Civil Service Examination in my second attempt and secured an All India Rank of 330. I graduated in Information Technology Engineering from Jabalpur Engineering College, Jabalpur, MP. My optional was History.

You can reach out to me on my e-mail: bajpai.aditya1292@gmail.com

Contents

Introduction

Congratulations on purchasing this book. This book is not intended to provide you with a detailed roadmap for studying for the exam. It is also not a book to boost your motivation. This book is an outcome of nearly 100+ questions that I have answered on Quora regarding civil services preparation. It is an attempt to provide clear insights to the aspirants on how to decide fundamental questions in the Civil Service exam preparation. Why choose Civil Services at all? What is your expectation from the service? Why not a private-sector job? Which service to choose? Is Delhi really important for preparation? Coaching vs Self-study? Should you give up your job? What exactly do you want from your life? These are some of the questions explored in this book. This is not your usual UPSC Book.

While interacting with the aspirants, I have realized that most of the aspirants are clueless as to what they expect from the service and on what criteria they choose a particular service. Further, the Civil Service exam is meant to select bright young officers who will administer the country in the years to come. But, if you see the statistics, the success rate in the Civil Service Exam is less than 1 percent. Year after year only the top 100 or 200 candidates enter the bureaucracy, the remaining are given another attempt. Precious years of youth are wasted in the exam process. If you clear the exam all is well, but if you don't, you are not left with enough options. So when should you stop? Is it worth it to continue? What is your motivation behind making repeated attempts? This book seeks to provide the answers to these questions.

This book also delves into the consequence of our choices and how it affects the entire bureaucratic machinery in the long run. The mismatch between expectations and reality, wants and needs, perks, and work of a civil servant can lead to disillusion, disenchantment, frustration and provide scope for slippage which might eventually lead to corruption. Therefore, a decision as simple as Why to Choose Civil Services is of a profound nature which the aspirants must give serious thought to.

Similar in consequence is the decision on choosing a particular service. Most of the time our decision to select a service stems mostly from what we have seen in films, read in books, seen on the ground, and told by others. Rarely is the choice well thought out with clear milestones and expectations from a service. What this neglect leads to is a sense of complacency and inefficiency in the overall working of a civil servant. Either he will be dissatisfied with the service or by the cadre. The dissatisfaction gradually clouds over all the aspects of one's being and results in slow and demotivated administration which plagues our country. Therefore, simple decisions of choosing the civil service and which service, in particular, can have a long-lasting impact on the overall administration.

The book doesn't provide any manual for studying. Everyone has their way. This book intends to provide overall clarity on the approach and what mistakes should be avoided while studying. How to stay motivated and how to stay relevant are some of the themes explored in this book.

One important aspect of civil service preparation is being financially independent which is always neglected. Even after repeated failure, aspirants continue to prepare while being financially dependent on someone else. Overall this impacts the course of study and also deprives youth of other opportunities which may be more suitable for them. The sense of "Holier than thou" which is ascribed to the civil services is somewhat problematic as it leads to youth wasting precious time and energy. Time to introspect is not given much importance and the process is such that by the time the final results are announced, the application form for next year is already filed which leaves little or no space for introspection.

Similarly, this book also focuses on the management of emotional intelligence which is affected because of shunning society in the process of studying. How does this affect the emotional quotient and one's ability to manage relations? This book takes a closer look at failure and explores what is it being a failure? Is the civil services exam everything? What motivates you to keep going or continuing?

In the end, the book seeks to encourage aspirants to believe in themselves and their abilities. Make studied choices and continue to skill oneself to stay relevant in the market. Decide when to seek employment and how to manage your study with the job. How to be a more positive human being and be a more productive and humane officer.

❑❑

PART-I

Why Civil Services?

Every year nearly a million or so aspirants apply for the Civil Services Exam and roughly 50 to 60 percent appear for the preliminary test. If you are reading this book, I am sure you consider yourself an aspirant. So this begets the cardinal question "Why do you want to join the Civil Services"? What is that you are looking for in the service and have you visualized your future? If no sudden answer comes to your mind then, relax, you are not the first.

Barring a few exceptions, aspirants are clueless as to why they want to join the Civil Services. Generally, the motivation to join the Civil Services is a combination of power, prestige, social status, willingness to serve the country, make a positive impact on society, financial stability, job satisfaction, social recognition, etc. So first and foremost, the motivation to join the Civil Services should be crystal clear in your mind.

Secondly, since the LPG reforms of 1991, the private sector has grown exponentially offering some of the most lucrative and challenging careers. If you compare the salary of a private sector employee and that of a civil servant in a similar position, the difference is vast and keeps growing with time. Further, a private-sector job also offers an opportunity to serve the public through other means. It may not be as direct as the civil services but still, the scope is there. So why have you not chosen a private-sector job?

Thirdly, the resources and manpower condition in the civil services is quite different from that of a private-sector job. Given the initial postings in rural or Tier-2 or 3 cities, managing personal life becomes increasingly tedious. It is no surprise that the divorce rate is one of the highest in the civil services and has increased over the period. Since the majority of the non-service spouses are in the private sector, the site location is mostly metro or Tier-1 city. Even for the couple who are in the civil services, a clash of ego and personalities leads to a breakdown in marriage. So have you taken these factors into account?

Fourthly, as you grow in your career, the initial zeal for public service and selfless motivation fades away. Power, prestige, and money subdue the judgment. And the difference between expectation and reality becomes increasingly stark. So you end up disinterested, disenchanted, and disillusioned. This disillusion is dangerous as it provides a slippage towards corruption. Therefore, your motivation behind choosing the civil services should be absolutely clear.

Finally, how you see yourself in the next five to ten years is very important. You may have cleared the exam. But this shouldn't stop the learning process. You must be updated with the latest developments. You must acquire the latest skill set as that will help you in your career. This chapter deals with all these issues.

❑❑

Chapter

1

What is Your Motivation?

For most of the aspirants, the motivation behind joining the civil services is primarily job security, a stable career, social recognition, power and authority, and the ability to make some positive change in society. The stability of a job is such a huge factor that even today a million or so aspirants prefer the Civil Services over the lucrative corporate job.

Your motivation plays a crucial role in determining your chances of success and also to propel your career over time. If your motivation is intrinsically materialistic then it will fade away sooner or later.

This is not some philosophical discourse but a ground reality. It is generally noted and observed that people who place a higher value on public service than monetary gratification, prefer working in the civil services. This is inherently linked to job satisfaction which will drive your career for years to come.

If you are motivated by the lure of power and prestige which comes with the civil services, then you are primarily guided by the perks of being a civil servant. "***Don't confuse the perks of being a civil servant with the work of a civil servant***". The perks offered to a civil servant are temporary. If you are attracted and attached to the perks of a civil servant, then you will develop a sense of entitlement. This is a dangerous slippage towards corruption and personal gratification.

Therefore, you must visualize your future not just in terms of your professional life but your personal life as well. What do you expect from the service and what are your ambitions? If they are perfectly aligned, you will have a harmonious career, if not, then the hustle will leave you frustrated.

Further, is the civil services the ultimate destination to which you have aspired for? No, but for most of the aspirants, this is the case. They have not visualized their career after entering the civil services.

Visualize Your Future

Clearing the Civil Services and lending your job is just a stepping stone towards your career. It is not the end but only the beginning. Generally, aspirants after clearing the exam become complacent. While preparing you were continuously in touch with all the latest happenings. But once you clear the exam, that motivation to continuously be abreast with the latest developments dwindles or fades away. The habit of reading newspapers takes a toll and the long working hours will keep you busy. So is this how you visualize your future? Was your planning limited only to clear the exam?

The twenty-first century bureaucracy demands you to be a service facilitator, and not just a service provider. The sense of lordship over the public which is a colonial mentality is not the case today. Governance is diversified. The scope and challenges of civil services are increasing every day. Civil servants, today are expected to be proactive and to walk that extra mile to deliver. The government and the public expect officers to be ready with the solutions.

More importantly, the civil services are linked to the public. You have to be a people's person. You need to interact with people, understand their problems, be sympathetic to their grievances and deliver them the services. Execution and public interaction are your primary job. If you are not a people's person and if you find no interest in going beyond your call of duty to redress the grievances, then maybe civil service is not your cup of tea.

Job Satisfaction

Despite all the constraints of working in public, job satisfaction is perhaps the key motivating factor that keeps you going. Being a part of the Customs Administration, I take pride and immense satisfaction in the work done during the Covid-19 pandemic. The speedy clearances by the Customs made vital medicines and equipment available in the country. In a way, howsoever, the small part I played, I am grateful that I could help in saving lives.

Despite all the hardships, the sheer satisfaction of public service makes a career in Civil Services so special. In 2017 I received a call in the afternoon. The complaint was against a boy who threatened the girl and her family with dire consequences. It was a case of dejected love. Though I was not in the police service, I assured the family of every possible help. The case was in Bangalore and little progress was made. After taking the information regarding FIR, I contacted the concerned police station and spoke directly with the inspector. Further, I talked to the Deputy Commissioner of police and also a few of my colleagues in IPS. It was the day I called and after a few hours, I received a call from the girl's family that the boy was arrested and his laptops and other devices through which he was threatening were confiscated. The girl was saved. This was the biggest satisfaction I had. I could save a life.

Day in and day out you work hard because you are serving the nation. This alone motivates you to aspire for the civil services. Not the perks or benefits but the sheer sense of public service is alone to get you going. Your service may take you to the remotest corner of the country to the corridors of power in the national capital. The opportunity to serve in such a diverse manner is perhaps the hallmark of the civil services. It enriches your life and prepares you to take undertake challenges.

So if you are motivated by the sense of public service and draw sheer satisfaction from it, then you have made the right choice. The key motivation to joining the Civil Services should be to serve the country in the widest possible manner. From the grass roots to the Secretariat, in whatever capacity. To use your power for the betterment of this country. To continuously learn and enhance your skills to make this country a better place for the present and future. Though this may sound very cliché-ridden, the fact remains this is the truth. When you have aspired to become a Civil Servant, you must carefully weigh your decision. Monetary benefits and an extravagant lifestyle shouldn't be your priority. Money will come, don't worry about it. Job satisfaction should be the guiding force.

❑❑

Chapter

2

Corporate Job vs Civil Services?

With the LPG reforms since 1991, the private sector in India has expanded exponentially. The work environment of any MNC is as challenging as it could be. With that, the perks of being in a comfortable office environment, with skilled staff, flexibility to switch careers, an acceptable standard of living, and manageable personal life, make the private-sector job much sought after. There is a much higher salary to take care of your needs. Who will not want such a job?

More importantly, it is not that only civil servants are doing their national duty. Many personalities in the private sector are doing a commendable job in serving the people. The mere fact that you pay your taxes and vote in an election is enough to show that you care for your nation.

You must seek a career after taking all these parameters into account. A government job is completely different from a private-sector job. You have human resource constraints, budgetary constraints, constant scrutiny, more pressure than your peers in the private sector, more accountability for your action, and tenuous working hours leading to imbalances in personal life. Added to it, your first posting may be in some rural setting. So, if there are so many problems with a private job, then why chose a career in the Civil Services?

To give you a better perspective, the overall work scenario, challenges and opportunities are discussed below so that you may make an informed choice.

Salary Comparison Between the Civil Services and a Corporate Job.

Keeping other factors constant, the salary between a government employee and a private sector employee could be classified into: (Indian Institute of Management, 2015)

1. **Person-Based**: This is the salary offered to an individual depending on the competency and skill set that the person brings to the work. This is widely prevalent in the private sector where the competition makes retention of skilled employees a necessity wherein competitive person-based income is offered.

2. **Pay for Performance:** This is the salary offered to an individual based on his/her performance. It is akin to the appraisal process in the private sector. In the government sector, though performance-based pay is not common, however, rewards and incentives are key drivers in many departments.

3. **Pay for the Position:** This is the salary offered to a particular range of positions held in an organization. It is usually further categorized into pay level and grade pay. It is generally the case with a government set up.

Therefore, you may see that in the private sector the skill set and competency play crucial roles but that is not the case with the government set up. In government, you are paid for the rank you hold.

Your competency may play some role in promotion and postings but overall it has minimal effect on the remuneration. However, to compare the civil service and a corporate job merely based on salary would be an injustice. The salary of a civil servant also comes with tangible and intangible benefits. You cannot put a price tag on social recognition, power, prestige, and authority enjoyed by a civil servant. Therefore, the comparison between the civil service and the corporate job should be on the following parameters.

Parameter	Civil Service	Corporate Job
1. Power and authority	Unparalleled power and authority.	More money but less power.
2. Technical knowledge and skill set	High in the initial years but stagnation creeps in as time goes by.	Continuous emphasis upon learning new skill and competencies.
3. Perks and benefits	Civil Services enjoys better perks and facilities like housing, telephones, car, security, etc.	Corporate jobs also have certain benefits but fewer and restricted as compared to civil services.

4.	Social prestige	Civil Servants enjoy remarkable social prestige which is really peerless.	Social prestige enjoyed by corporate jobs is less compared to civil servants.
5.	Diversity of Career	Civil servants work in diverse fields ranging from rural development to national security, international relations, trade and commerce to energy security, defence, art and culture, etc.	In a corporate job, your domain is much more restricted because of the specialized nature of the job and skill set associated with it.
6.	Work Experience	Civil Servants handle more work pressure, much bigger manpower and larger projects from early years on. Adding the resource	Corporate job comes with its own set of work experience which is equally rewarding. However, the work

	crunch to it, civil servants learn to work in any work environment and deliver results.	environment is certainly better, staff is better skilled and resources are at easy disposal.
7. Restricted job profile	Civil servants have little flexibility to switch the organization. However, it is more or less compensated by a diverse work profile.	Switching of organization is relatively much easier and more flexible.
8. Job security	Civil Servants are constitutionally protected and enjoy superior job security and stability as compared to any private organization.	Job security is less and more or less related to the global economic scenario and competencies.

9.	Accountability	Civil Servants are custodians of public trust in the system. Therefore, they are more accountable for their actions.	A person in a corporate job is not directly accountable to the public and therefore, the scrutiny and accountability are less.
10.	Job satisfaction	Civil Services offer one of the highest job satisfaction across all the careers in the country.	Job satisfaction is less as compared to the civil services.

Specialized vs Generalized Nature of Job

One of the arguments often stated against the Civil Services is that they are generalized services with little domain expertise and this somewhat contributes to red-tapism, which slows down the pace of the country's development. This becomes all the more relevant in light of new challenges like Global Warming, Energy Efficiency, Artificial Intelligence, Cryptocurrency, Machine Learning, Cyberspace, the Internet of Things, etc. It is generally believed that the private sector is much more skilled to undertake such challenges.

Further many jobs are threatened by the technological onslaught and therefore, the relevance of generalized professions like the civil services is questioned. We are also generally taught that to survive in a complex and highly competitive world, we need to narrow down on certain specialized career choices. Having said that, it becomes quite obvious that the future lies with specialized jobs like the ones in the corporate sector. Should you take this into account while choosing between the civil services and a corporate job?

Psychologists Daniel Kahneman and Gary Klein independently conducted several studies to find that there is no substantial correlation between experience and expertise. The key factor that determines whether or not experience will inevitably lead to expertise is the domain in question. (Klein, 2009). Several studies have shown that experience and repetition simply do not create an improved performance or learning in a real-world scenario. Successful adapters have a range. They are excellent at avoiding cognitive entrenchment and taking knowledge from one pursuit and applying it creatively to another. Specialization, therefore, is not a good idea in domains where patterns rarely occur. For instance, administrative work like civil service requires you to broaden your area of operation and therefore, with experience decide your domain of specialization. Challenges are not defined and rules of operation are not rigid. Therefore, having range can put you ahead in such a world. (Epstein, 2019)

Further, the civil services provide ample opportunities to nurture your skillset with experience. The debate between generalists and specialists therefore should apply where the domain is rigid, skill sets are well defined, rules are restricted and parameters are specified. In a job where none of these factors apply, you have to be a generalist. More importantly, the civil service puts you in a leadership position where you have to decide on a wide variety of matters which requires a breadth of understanding. Tunnel vision, which is often associated with specialization may not work at all times. Therefore, choose according to your preference taking these parameters into account.

Twenty-First Century Bureaucracy

Having considered all the parameters of comparison between the civil services and a corporate job, you must understand that bureaucracy today is not what it used to be. We no longer live in the nineteenth century. While anonymity and neutrality are still cherished virtues, it is hard to practise in the twenty-first century. The dawn of social media and speedy grievance redress mechanism means that officers often have to be on social media, discuss government programmes, create awareness, solve problems, take feedback and be proactive.

Therefore, today's bureaucracy provides a much larger avenue of public interaction across all services. Social recognition is also now much wider. An important consequence of it is that today officers can walk that extra mile and also showcase their work. While this is debatable in the context of anonymity in bureaucracy. Still, it provides some avenues of personal enterprise which was earlier restricted only to the private-sector job. It has also led to many innovative ways of public service. Take, for instance, Mr. Armstrong Pame, an IAS officer who was able to construct a 100 kilometre road without any help from the government, primarily making use of social media.

Also, when it comes to acquiring new skills government encourages and also provides many platforms for skill development for officers. Therefore, all that is needed is the zeal and the passion in the officer and the urge to keep growing. Bureaucracy today is more dynamic, open, and gradually becoming more skill-oriented. While naysayers may believe that the civil services are losing their charm against the onslaught of new technology, I believe it is the best time to be in the government, challenges are new, exposure is more, the opportunity for personal and professional growth is immense.

❑❑

Chapter 3

Issues and Challenges

Balancing personal and professional life becomes a challenge in the civil services. The spectrum of challenges in the services is unique and different from that of a corporate job. Some of these are discussed below:

1. **Transfers**: Transfers in the civil services are frequent. The transfer may be for whatever reason but it completely affects the personal life of an officer. The problem becomes all the more challenging when you have a working spouse and your place of posting may not

be suitable for your partner. Since transfers happen periodically, it poses a challenge in family planning.

2. **Political Interference:** This affects the overall work environment. Further, it interferes with the neutrality of the officer and affects the transfers, postings, and sometimes even promotions.

3. **Recognition**: As already discussed, officers in government are paid for the rank and position they hold. That means any kind of additional skill acquired or extraordinary work done will not lead to more remuneration, unless it is some reward. Therefore, recognition of excellence is somewhat less compared to a corporate job.

4. **Corruption**: Corruption in the public sector is widely prevalent which is a known fact. The officer has to deal with it, overcome it and suitably motivate his subordinate for not indulging in it. In a way, you have to lead by your conduct.

5. **Marital Life**: The Divorce rate among officers is quite high and is increasing. The primary

reason is the hectic work schedule with less personal time. If your spouse is in the private sector, then it becomes more difficult because the workplace is different. If both the spouses are in service, then the ego clash is another challenge.

6. **Public Perception**: You will hear frequently that "officers are corrupt", "bureaucracy is lazy", "officers have ruined the country", etc., Despite the majority of officers being honest and diligent, public perception remains the same and it somewhat hurts your sentiments as well. However hard you work, public perception changes very slowly.

7. **Excessive Scrutiny**: As an officer, you are under constant scrutiny and often an honest mistake is confused with deliberate misconduct. You will be motivated to perform but somewhere at the back, you will be scared of the risk associated with honest performance. Gradually some officers yield to these threats and become complacent while others struggle. Either way, the efficiency of bureaucracy gets affected.

8. **Factions**: In government, due to historical reasons and the overall construction of the system, factions based on caste, language, region, and religion are formed. These factions are often influential and frequently, an officer bends to the wishes of such factions. This you will not encounter in any MNC where the very cosmopolitan nature reduces the scope of formation of such groups.

9. **Expectation vs Reality**: The life of a civil servant is not what you see in movies. It is not what you read in books. It is like any other job with somewhat more operational diversity and social recognition. It is not like a car with *all batti* can stop the traffic and put citizens in awe. It doesn't happen. If you don't follow traffic rules, you pay a fine.

10. **Career Switch:** Switching a career in the Civil Services is not possible. You enter after clearing the exam. But you can't leave it and return to it. You may change the department, you may change the station, or you may change the ministry but in the end, you will be in government. The ease of switching jobs for career progression is not the case with the Civil Services.

Beyond Money, Why Do People Choose to be a Civil Servant?

Money is just one kind of wealth. Having said that, it is worth mentioning that wealth is multifaceted. A good family, a healthy life, close friends, and people who love you are all part of your wealth. One important aspect of wealth, particularly in the Indian context, is social prestige and power to bring positive changes in people's lives.

That being the case, the Civil Services provides the platform to achieve both – social prestige and power. Group A/Class I officers of the Central Government are heads of their respective departments and are in a way instrumental in policy planning and policy execution. This provides an opportunity to help people on the widest possible scale. Giving an example from my own experience, I am a 2016 batch officer, in 2018 I was the Assistant Commissioner of Bijapur, Karnataka. The same year I was also made Nodal officer for MSMEs development of Bagalkot District. In that capacity, I had first-hand interaction with handloom workers of the famed Ilkal saris. I am from Madhya Pradesh, but I got a chance to visit and explore the rural hinterlands of Northern Karnataka.

In the year 2019, I spearheaded a chase operation of a truck carrying illicit goods. The chases lasted several hours but they gave me first-hand experience in law enforcement and challenges at a practical level. The kick you get from such an operation; the adrenaline rush is unparalleled. Therefore, your experience is not limited to anyone's domain. During the Covid-19 pandemic, it is the vast network of officers in the services that presented a joint front to tackle the crisis head-on. We were all attending to our day-to-day duties but at the same time, we helped people through whatever means we could. And the satisfaction of contributing whatever we can to save lives cannot be expressed in words. In the Civil Services, you interact with people from all walks of life. In a way, it all adds to your personality and overall richness of life. The diversity of job profiles never makes your life dull. You always have some new challenges each day. The Civil Services give you the satisfaction of serving your country and your people. At the risk of repeating, job satisfaction in the Civil Services is the real driving force.

❑❑

Chapter

4

What to Look for in a Service

It is a fact that nearly 95 percent of the aspirants sit for the Civil Service Exam only to become an IAS officer. Many are inspired by the charm of District Collector. The power, the prestige which comes with the job. But are you cut out for it? While preparing for any corporate job, we are clear as to what domain we want, what skill set is required, where we see ourselves in the next 5 years, and, what are the challenges we are going to face. But when it comes to government jobs why do we ignore all these parameters?

It is a hard reality that only a few aspirants know why they want to become an IAS or IPS officer. Few have just binged on Singham Universe and made their choice. Many are completely unaware that there are 21 other services as well. One who doesn't get the desired service will cry for a better service, the person in a better service will cry for a better cadre. Therefore, crying continues unless you decide what exactly you want. So how do you choose a service?

There are the following parameters that will help you choose:

1. **Recognition of Effort**: Your work in your service should be recognized not just by your peers in the organization but even by society to provide that deep sense of satisfaction. You must not confuse societal recognition as an antithesis to the concept of anonymity of bureaucracy. Both are different. Your work must be acknowledged. This is a driving force to perform better each time. Recognition and motivation are directly correlated.

2. **Chance for Useful Contribution**: Your service must provide you with ample opportunities to make a useful contribution. This may not be restricted only to the job at hand but to the

overall system. For instance, a simple act of digitizing the file system of your office is a great contribution not just to improving the efficiency of administration but to reducing pollution.

3. **Opportunities to Use and Develop Skills**: Once you have cracked the Civil Service Exam, your journey begins. For many aspirants, it is the end of the struggle. But in reality, it is the beginning. Your service must provide you opportunities to constantly upgrade your skill to stay relevant in the market.

4. **Congenial Work Environment**: A good and healthy work environment goes a long way in improving the performance of any department. No matter how great is your work profile, if the work environment is not healthy or conducive, it will be overall detrimental. Further, as you grow, a congenial work environment adds to your confidence and overall personality.

5. **Challenging Opportunities at Work**: Challenges are the building block of your professional and personal life. Without challenges, your work will be mundane and gradually you

will lose interest in the work. Therefore, don't run away from challenges but face them and overcome them.

6. **The Right Level of Authority**: Clearing the Civil Service Exam and not enjoying authority is futile. Your service must give you the discretion to apply your skillset. Authority to use power for good and make some positive change is the fundamental reason why anyone opts for the Civil Services.

Based on these parameters, overall job satisfaction is achieved. The 2010 Civil Services Survey by the Department of Personnel and Training (DoPT) provides the following interesting picture regarding job satisfaction in various services.

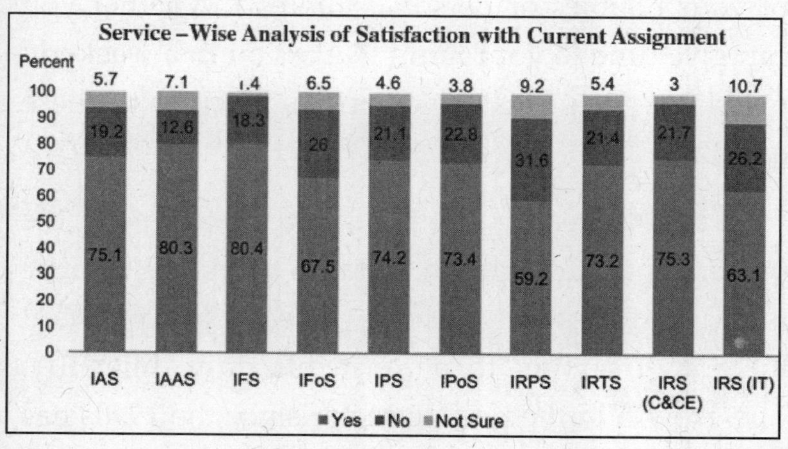

Managing Personal and Professional Life:

While initially, the zeal for social transformation oozes out from every pore of your being, as you grow you realize that the system moves slowly. Reforms happen but take time. Rules are binding. You are constantly being scrutinized by society, media, judiciary, vigilance, etc. The burning zeal paves the way for pragmatism and sometimes complacency.

Therefore, the service you choose should offer you some discretion and authority. It must give you ample scope of growth professionally and personally as well. While most of us are concerned about planning our career milestones, it is equally important to give sufficient thought to personal life. Whether you can take time for the development of your hobbies or personal interest? Whether you can give time to your family? Are you in a weekend marriage? You must give serious thought to these questions.

It is a sad reality that the divorce rate among the officers is quite high which takes work-life balance for a toss. A peaceful home is equally important for a civil servant to perform his duty diligently. The growth in the private sector since the 1990s has created many employment opportunities. While most corporate jobs are concentrated in metros, an All India Service Officer begins his/her career from a rural background. Given this, maintaining the work-life balance becomes important. Not only that, but inter-service marriages are also not easy given the clash of egos and tenuous job profile.

Therefore, all these factors must be kept in mind while deciding on a service. But most importantly, you must have the right attitude and aptitude for the job.

❑❑

Chapter

5

The Disillusioned Civil Servant

You enter as a bright young officer, ambitious to change the system. All you care about is public service. However gradually the shine of prestige, money, and power clouds your motivation. And what you started as and what you end up being is completely different. As a civil servant, you are required to deal with people. If dealing with people, being empathetic to their problems, providing solutions to their grievances, and being innovative in your approach is not your cup of tea then the Civil

Services is not for you. And it's fine. It is always better to do what you like instead of what is the norm.

If a comparison could be drawn between the salary of a civil servant and a corporate job in the same hierarchy, the salary of the latter is better. Now, why is this important? Simply for the reason that as you grow, the difference in salary also grows. So when you see your friends in corporate jobs having foreign vacations, buying luxury cars, houses, etc., you will be disillusioned. This disillusion will either provoke you to change your career path or be corrupt. In either case, you will not be doing justice to your job. Today the problem plaguing our country is the disillusioned civil servant. When expectations don't match reality, it leads to frustrations and dissatisfaction.

Therefore, your motivation to choose a career in the civil services should be crystal clear. Why have you joined the service? If monetary gratification and a luxurious life are your prime concern, then the civil services are not for you. This job expects you to do public service. You are the custodian of public trust in the system and therefore, your integrity and commitment to service should be unconditional. Any kind of expectation for such a job is detrimental to the overall requirement of the work.

Further, the disillusion is not only limited to comparison with your peers in a corporate job. Disillusion also sets in when you often see an honest mistake is gravely punished. You will see that however zealous you are; the system takes its own time to change. So why shouldn't you take sides? The moment you do so, you have done away with neutrality. A bias of any kind is harmful to public service. You cannot choose whom to deliver, whom to punish and whom to protect. You are here to do your duty.

The fact remains that we all crave recognition. It may be on social media, turning bureaucrats into influencers, or it may be in your work. It may also be in your social circle. The sense of entitlement that comes with the civil services is dangerous. As I mentioned earlier, never confuse the perks of a civil servant with his work. Never assume that the privileges associated with the rank are your right. Nothing is permanent. More importantly, the more you crave attention the more you boost your ego and the more unapproachable you become. As a civil servant, you are expected to deal with people and you have to be approachable to understand their problems.

So what should be your motivation to choose the civil services. In simple words, your motivation should be public service, national development, and commitment to your duty. It is as the Bhagavad Gita says *"Nishkam Karm"*. Do your duty with the utmost sense of commitment to the nation and its people. The rest will be taken care of. After the 7th Pay Commission, the salary of a civil servant is quite satisfactory and enough to take care of your needs. All you have to do is rein in your desires.

Decide for yourself after taking all these factors into account and then appear for the exam. The country needs honest, courageous, and committed officers. Be one and be proud.

Key Takeaways

The purpose of this chapter is to encourage you to make a clear choice regarding your career. You may choose a corporate job or the civil services. But whatever you choose make an informed choice with full conviction. To do so you must ask yourself what do you expect from your career and your life? And does your career choice align with your life plans? You must rein in your expectations when you decide to sit for the exam. Your motivation to join the civil services must be inherently driven by the spirit of public service. Nothing less will do.

If you have decided to go ahead with the civil services exam, the next chapter will guide you on how to prepare. What mistakes you must avoid and how you can better manage your time.

❑❑

PART II

How to "Actually" Prepare for the Civil Services

The Civil Services Exam has acquired such a divine status in our country that mere mentioning of its preparation evokes inspiration and sometimes ridicule. Whether you have decided to prepare for this exam or not, one fact must be kept in mind always – ***It is just an exam.*** Yes, it will get you into Group A positions in the Central Government but that's it. It is just a job like others.

Now, why am I telling you this? It is because you are preparing for an exam which offers a government job. Being a government servant, your job is to execute and administer government policies. Your job is not to be associated with them or advertise yourself. By doing so, you are interfering with the original motivation of joining the Civil Services which is – service to the nation and its people. Therefore, start the preparation for the exam but don't advertise it. Keep your preparation to yourself. ***Prepare in the dark and strike like a thunderbolt*.**

Another very important point is that just by getting into premiere coaching institutions, you are not guaranteeing your success. I have seen many aspirants, getting over-confident and flaunting expensive bags offered by these institutes as a mark of guaranteed success. Believe me, most of the students in the institutes are not serious aspirants. Your competition is only with those 15,000 – 20,000 students who will clear the prelims. Focus on that. Don't get bogged down by the sheer number of aspirants. It doesn't matter. Let a million or so fill the form, only 50 percent will appear for the exam and only 2 percent to 5 percent will be actually, dedicatedly, and seriously preparing for the exam.

Should you take coaching or not? Well, that depends on your capability and understanding of the exam. The decision is personal and must be guided by certain parameters. However, it is not a must to take coaching. People clear this exam through self-study as well. So stop following the myths associated with the exam, which I am sure will encounter throughout your journey.

How you should prepare for the exam is your personal choice. You must seek guidance from toppers but you must not blindly follow them. Their journey is different. The kind of obstacles you encounter is unique to you. Therefore, focus on yourself. If you like an optional then go for it. Don't listen to what others say or how others react. How does it matter? Are you becoming an IAS officer for others or yourself? Listen to others but follow what suits you best.

In this part I will address various issues which aspirants encounter like – coaching or self-study, Delhi or home, choosing an optional, getting started, the importance of basic textbooks, a systematic approach to the exam, and keeping the right motivation throughout the process. I will also dispel many myths in the process. This part will also address the common mistakes committed by the aspirants and how you must avoid them.

Chapter

6

Coaching vs Self-Study

The coaching industry is a billion-dollar enterprise. On average reputed coaching institutes for the civil services charge somewhere between ₹ 1.5 to ₹ 2 lakhs from every aspirant. Some of the institutes claim to have thousands of aspirants enrolled. This is not just limited to New Delhi. Even in other bigger cities, new coaching centres have mushroomed claiming to produce new toppers every year. Every institute claims to have produced hundreds of toppers every year. Those numbers never add up. Yet each year, enamoured by the inspiring images and advertisements, lakhs of students enrol again.

Coaching is not the correct term. Nobody can coach a person in his late twenties on how to study. You have reached this far which means you know how to study. The only thing you need is guidance. Therefore, what you need is mentoring. But before that, have you evaluated yourself? Why do you need coaching? What are the areas where you need guidance? Do you need complete guidance or selective? On what basis have you evaluated yourself. Let's answer these questions first.

Do a Self-Analysis

To decide whether to take coaching or not, you must analyse your strengths and weaknesses. Get comfortable with the syllabus and exam pattern. Do a proper survey of past years' papers, and resources available to you. Generally speaking, people start studying for this exam even before looking at the syllabus. And then they will glorify and romanticize it by saying ***"everything under the sun is the syllabus of the UPSC"***. Nothing is farther from the truth. The Civil Service Exam has a well-defined syllabus with clear expectations from the aspirants. And despite this, aspirants hardly study the syllabus and give it the respect that it deserves.

The evolving nature of questions and the change in syllabus since 2013 has made the process very dynamic. You are no longer asked "*When did the First Battle of Panipat take place*?" The focus is on "*Why Babur won the First Battle of Panitpat despite the superior strength of the Lodhis*?" The static part of the syllabus has remained more or less the same, the emphasis is now upon the analytical ability of the candidate. It is in this background that one must see the requirement of coaching or self-study.

In many institutes, the emphasis on methodologies is still on the pre-2013 exam pattern. Therefore, take the syllabus and past year papers and then strategise. Today, all the details you need are available online free of cost. You can subscribe to free tutorials and YouTube videos and get all the necessary information for the process. So analyse your competency and then decide. If you still require coaching, then opt for it.

Delhi vs Home

When I first came to Delhi, even I went to ORN and was simply charmed by the environment. Minutes later, I was intimidated by the same. Lakhs of students studying around me, each minute I am being compared to someone else, my performance being measured, judged, and analysed. Given the sheer dynamism in the environment, I was both awestruck and demotivated. While at my home I was isolated, in Delhi for the first time I saw the real competition.

I even planned to rent a room in ORN but seeing the overall environment, I decided to give it a miss. I enrolled in coaching and paid nearly ₹ 1 lakh. In the coaching the pedagogy was outdated. The methodology was not much use after the 2013 changes in the exam. After nearly 2-3 months of enrolling, I left the coaching centre. I stayed in Noida due to my job in TCS and continued my preparation from there.

On average, in 2015 the rent of a single room was approximately ₹ 8,000 to 10,000. The first room which the broker offered me in ORN had no ventilation. I had to share that room with 4 other aspirants. I am sure the rent must have increased and so is the cost of food, clothing, and other necessities. So is it required? For an exam that costs less than ₹ 500/- there is no requirement to shell out lakhs of rupees for coaching, lodging, and boarding in Delhi or any metro city for that matter. All you need is motivation and Wi-Fi.

The primary reason for coming to Delhi is coaching. And as I already stated, coaching for the UPSC is not a must and is overhyped. You are competing only against 15,000-20,000 serious candidates, scattered all across the country. Therefore, if you can meet all your study requirements in your hometown, then there is no need for going to a new city and setting up a temporary stay, meeting the cost of expensive lodging and boarding. Whatever you do, must add value to your preparation.

So decide for yourself. If need be, go to Delhi, live among the aspirants, and compete, but don't squander this opportunity because time wasted will not return. And don't fall for the "aspirant syndrome" wherein, a person takes pleasure in being an aspirant. He/she enjoys debating the policy decision of the government in ORN. In the process, he/she turns more and more political. And the purpose for which he/she came to Delhi is lost. He/she ends up being an activist. Negativity creeps in and a disillusioned person comes out of Delhi. This is not what we want.

If you are interested in going to Delhi, then by all means go. But your decision should be guided only from the exam perspective. You are not there for an extended holiday with your friends. A mistake many aspirants commit. The lack of accountability affects your study. The sooner you realize the better.

Studying in your home or any place for that matter where you are comfortable, will help you avoid unnecessary expenses. Moreover, you will avoid useless market gossip related to UPSC which will help you to focus better. I chose history as optional not knowing whether it is good or bad. I just loved it and so I took it and excelled in it. If I had listened to market gossip, I would not be writing this book. At your home, you will be more focused on your study as there will be a comfortable environment.

❑❑

Chapter 7

Some Common Doubts

I have often met aspirants who are confused about which mode is better. As long as the mode helps your study it is better. It doesn't matter whether you are studying online or offline. It is strictly a personal choice. I for one, am quite comfortable with the online mode as it allows me the flexibility of time management and note editing. I do not have to carry all my books.

Today nearly all the books are available in PDF format for free. Video lectures and tutorials are available online. There are dedicated WhatsApp and

Telegram groups for UPSC Civil Service preparation which provides a good forum for debating and discussing all the issues and challenges. Honestly, online services have expanded so much in the last couple of years, that anyone can prepare for this exam from the comfort of their homes.

Further, for working professionals who cannot attend physical classes, the online mode is best as it provides you the flexibility to use your time in the best possible manner. Therefore, take all these factors into account and make a studied decision. There are two categories of aspirants. One, who are beginners, who have just started. The other one is the veterans who have spent a few years. This chapter is for beginners. The issues faced by the veterans will be discussed in the last part of the book.

As a beginner, get the first thing in mind and I think I have repeated it again and again—this is just an exam and just another government job. Therefore, if you think that you may choose a graduation subject that aligns with your aspirations to crack the civil service exam, you are wrong.

Today the environment is not what it used to be in the 1990s or even till the early 2000s. Today, you need to be marketable. Your skills must be multi-dimensional and must be used from a wider perspective. Therefore, don't restrict your graduation only to the Civil Service Exam.

Your graduation subject must have built a foundation for your career if the Civil Service is no longer an option. Therefore, choose carefully taking into account the changing scenario of the global economy and employability. This is not to say that you must have a plan B. This is to emphasize that your skillset should be such that it could be deployed in both the public and private sector as and when the need be. Today, lateral entry at Deputy and Joint Secretary levels provides an opportunity to work at the senior level in government. Therefore, develop a market-oriented skillset. This will not only help you in government but also in the larger perspective.

In this chapter, I will discuss some of the doubts which must be clear in your mind before you begin your journey and even during the journey. For that whatever is best for you must be done.

Postgraduation or Civil Service – Which Should be Attempted First?

I get this question a lot especially from engineers as to whether they should do M.Tech or MBA first and then opt for the Civil Service Exam? The answer to this question depends on your priority and your vision. Doing a Master's is a great advancement in your education but what utility does it have for your career in the Civil Services? If you are planning to have a Master's as a second option or backup plan then you are committing two fundamental mistakes.

First, you are wasting precious years. Say, you graduated at the age of 23. You devote 2 full years to your Master's so you start your preparation at the age of 25. You have lost 2 years which you could have used for the Civil Services. Now once you are done with your Masters, if you clear the exam next year, it is great. But, if not, then if you are still preparing for the Civil Service, it means that you are wasting not just your time but also a great skill set that you acquired in your masters. It will not be used in the Civil Services, so what was the purpose of all this?

Second, you are pursuing a failed dream. You have already decided on the Civil Services and now you are keeping your Masters as a backup plan. When you have such an approach, you become careless with your preparation. Whenever you feel down, instead of making an extra effort, you will take comfort in the fact that you have a good backup.

This is a recipe for failure not for success. You are neither passionate about the Civil Services nor your Master's.

More importantly, you will get a chance to pursue a Master's once you are in the service. The government provides ample opportunities to pursue the higher education of your choice. There may be some aspirants who after completing the Masters decide to appear for the Civil Service Exam. In this case, the decision is made during or after the Master's. It was not made during graduation. So learn to value the importance of time and prioritize your future accordingly.

Preparing with Backups: Preparing for Failure

Many aspirants start their Civil Services Preparation keeping backup options like SSC, State PSC, Bank PO, RBI, etc., While this provides a sense of security and stability, this approach has its drawbacks. Let's say you can devote 10-12 hours of study. In that, you give 70 percent time to UPSC and the rest to other exams. Now imagine competing against an aspirant who is devoting 100 percent of 10-12 hours of study only for UPSC. Who has a better probability of success?

The syllabus of the UPSC is vast and it requires a minimum of one and a half years of dedicated study simply to cover the syllabus. If you devote the same time to other exams, you will not be able to cover the syllabus and develop confidence. Secondly, as I stated earlier, preparing with backup provides you with a sense of security which makes you complacent and reduces the effort in the long run, which is detrimental to the study.

You must decide for backup when you have failed for two consecutive attempts, not from the beginning. Avoid the temptation of stability and security from the start. It will limit your capability to take the risk and go that extra mile which makes all the difference. Make up your mind on what you want to do. Do not gamble. The one thing which I have seen in aspirants who clear the exam is the sheer will to clear it. They don't settle for anything less than what they have aspired for. So shouldn't you. Do not fear the uncertainty of the exam. Give your best.

What is the Right Age to Start the Preparation?

This is one of the most common questions. Understand the dynamics first. You must get selected as early as possible to reach the highest ranks in bureaucracy. The promotion in bureaucracy is mostly in terms of seniority. Although there are some exceptions to this rule. But more or less, this is the prevalent norm. So the early you enter, the late you retire.

But having said this, don't listen to the myth that *"UPSC is biased against older candidates"*. Had this been the case, many top rankers would not have secured such ranks in their thirties. Statistically, the average age of candidates clearing this exam is 27 years. (26.9 to be precise). Most of the candidates fall under the age bracket of 26 to 28 years. One inherent advantage of being slightly older is that a person tends to be more mature in handling such a complicated job. However, this is not true in all cases.

So when should one start preparing for this exam? Ideally, one should start one and a half years before appearing in the exam. One and a half year is sufficient to build your foundation and give you ample time to practise and revise. Having said that, the best time is if you could begin with your graduation. Your mind is fresh and you have the maximum chance to secure a good rank. With time, your chances to secure a good rank diminishes mainly because your motivation level goes down.

Importance of NCERT

You must begin your preparation by NCERT. They are the standard textbooks that are readily available across the length and breadth of the country. They are easy to understand and will clear your basics. They are written by eminent authors like R.S. Sharma, Bipin Chandra, Satish Chandra, etc. and most importantly, direct questions have come from NCERT. Therefore, their importance cannot be undermined. In a way, you have to repeat your schooling from the 6th to the 12th again.

As a thumb rule, don't select any book which is more than 300 pages for preparing the preliminary (this doesn't apply to Lakshmi Kant). Don't go for BA or MA level books. Trust the process and begin from the basics. You need to know sufficient enough to clear the exam. You are not here to do a PhD. This should be clear in your mind. You aim to crack the exam that's it. Nothing more and nothing less.

You may get a booklist from various sources but stick to basics and only if the need arises then go for higher-level textbooks. Make use of technology and use whatever media is available to you to make notes and understand the concept. As far as note-making is concerned. do what is best for you. If you are comfortable with online notes, then go for it else, subscribe to hardcopy notes.

How to Choose the Optional?

The next big step is to decide on your option. Don't listen to market rumours. No optional is good or bad. No optional is favoured by the examiners. No optional is scoring. All optional are equally good and bad. The foremost criteria to choose an option should be your interest in the subject. You cannot assume to score well in anthropology if your interest lies in philosophy. You have to put your heart into the subject, therefore, you must love that subject. Don't bother about what everyone else is saying. Listen to your heart.

While studying for the General Studies you would have already studied some of the optional in brief. So choose the one which intrigues you. To choose an optional, look out for syllabus and past year papers. I picked up history as optional even though I am from a science background. I had an interest in the subject. I never listened to the market. I had no idea whether it is a good or bad option. I just knew that I love it and I scored pretty well. But decide your optional as fast as you can. A dedicated time of 6 to 8 months is required for an optional and therefore have sufficient time to study and revise it.

Some of the parameters that you can keep in mind while deciding the optional are:

1. Your interest in the subject
2. Alignment with your academic background
3. Availability of study material
4. Availability of coaching institute, if required
5. Performance of the subjects in the last couple of years

But do keep in mind, that your interest in the subject is of vital importance. The other parameters will fail if you have no interest in the subject. Further, study to crack the exam, you are not here to do a PhD as I stated earlier. Your aim must be crystal clear.

Is UPSC Not for the Average People?

I cleared the UPSC despite having a very average academic background. So have the others. People are even clear despite having suffered a failure in their academics. Till my second year in college, I didn't even know what I had to do in life. And this is normal. All that is needed is the perseverance to clear the exam.

As per UPSC's notification, if you have secured 55 percent or more in graduation then you are eligible for the exam. Average people do clear this exam with flying colours. If you see the eligibility condition of the notification, you will find that intelligence is not the condition. All that is needed is that you secure 55 percent in graduation. Pretty average isn't it? Moreover, even in the interview or personality test, a candidate's mental calibre is judged. So it is all about general awareness of your surroundings, national and international scenario, and ability to analyse the problem and provide its solution.

Is Life Settled After the Civil Service Exam?

Though a certain level of job security and stability does come after clearing the exam, nearly, all the aspirants think that their struggle ends with the exam. This is not true. It is just the beginning. In such a huge system, now you have to leave your mark and make those changes which you always dreamt about.

Moreover, after clearing the exam, only some 200-300 odd candidates do not appear again for the exam.

So life is not settled for the rest of the candidates. Even those who get their desired service will crave for the desired cadre or some better rank. Many will crave the home cadre. So this endless pursuit of what you need will continue.

On top of that, the challenges of working in a government set up have their own set of challenges. Frequent transfers, politicisation, corruption, manpower shortage, lack of skilled workforce, resource crunch, excessive scrutiny, public exposure, etc., presents their own set of problems in some services. Therefore, you need to find your way in the bureaucracy.

❑❑

Chapter

8

Balance Your Life

The process of this exam is so tedious that often aspirants are not able to balance their personal life. Preparing for the Civil Services affects aspirants mentally, physically, emotionally, financially, socially, and psychologically. Since most of the aspirants are cut off from the outside world, they do not have the necessary social conduit to release the built-up stress and anxiety. There are cases of emotional breakdowns. Many of them turn to heavy drinking and smoking. Being under such depression, in the prime of your youth tells that something is not correct with the way you are preparing for this exam.

Adding to it is the mental construct that the Civil Services exam requires you to sacrifice everything. You are so emotionally disconnected from the outside world that eventually it affects your emotional health. We are social animals and we crave society. Your job will require you to interact with people, understand their problems and provide the solution. If at the stage of preparation itself, you are under such anxiety what will happen to you once you clear the exam? The workload will increase manifold and so is the stress. How will you manage that?

The social cost of this exam is huge. Lakhs of candidates stay unemployed till 28-30 years of age for preparing for the exam. And this unemployment is forced. You have the necessary skills but you choose to be unemployed. What this results in is that you are financially dependent on someone else. You are not in control of your life's decisions. Once you fail to clear in 4-5 attempts the stress and anxiety of being jobless will grip your mind. You will not be peaceful and will not be able to devote your 100 percent to this exam.

This forced unemployment puts pressure not just on your life but also on your family and your relationships. You have stopped certain aspects of your life which should have gone naturally with the age. This adds negatively to your study. Lord Buddha preached the middle path. A path between severe asceticism and materialism. Learn and apply it in your exam life.

Should You Quit Your Job?

Everybody says the UPSC is the toughest exam in the country so I must give it 100 percent therefore I must give up my job and dedicate my full time to it. This is not required. As I stated earlier, you need to devote one and a half years of serious preparation to build your foundation. But after that, you must seek financial independence to relieve your mind of stress.

The exam process is built to check the mental calibre of the candidate. A working professional exudes more confidence and awareness than his/her peer. Moreover, if you have crossed 25-26 years of age, even the society expects you to be working. This has some advantages in the personal interview as well. You give an impression that you are in control of your life and are earning and supporting your family. Many committees have also recommended lowering the age of exams primarily to reduce the social cost of this 'forced unemployment'.

As Group A officers, you will be leading people and will be working on multiple tasks that too with a calm and composed mind. Therefore, it is possible to study while working. Every year many candidates successfully clear the exam while working. Hence, seek a remunerative job and be independent. In this way, you can decide the course of your study according to you. Take control of your life.

Should You Sacrifice Your Personal Life?

No, you shouldn't. Even if you are preparing in Delhi and living alone. You must not sacrifice your personal life. I will try to make the point through research conducted in this field. The Self Determination Theory (Ryan and Deci, 2017) is a theory of human motivation that highlights an individual's innate tendency towards growth and development. Associated to it is the Basic Psychological Needs Theory which establishes three needs central to well-being:

1. **Autonomy**: Need to fully endorse one's action.

2. **Competence**: Need to experience growth and mastery.

3. **Relatedness**: Need to feel the reciprocal connection and care with other people.

When you cut yourself off from society, you sacrifice the three basic needs of psychological well-being. For instance, aspirants may limit their sense of personal volition and choice as they feel forced to study to complete tasks they feel are necessary for meeting the demands of their programme – ***a sacrifice of autonomy***. They may also avoid opportunities for growth that do not directly contribute to their career – ***a sacrifice of competence***. Finally, aspirants may lock themselves away with their books, isolating themselves from human connection – ***a sacrifice of relatedness***. When self-initiated, these sacrifices affect wider psychological aspects of life.

"The road to pursuing a long-term career goal is not without its trials and tribulations. People are constantly forewarned that they must be willing to make sacrifices to achieve the goals that they hold most dear, and are often encouraged to do so. Indeed, social media is fraught with memes and quotes asserting that, "If you don't sacrifice for what you want, what you want becomes the sacrifice".

We find that such potential words of wisdom must be interpreted with caution. Indeed, the relation between sacrificing physical needs and desirable activities with making greater goal progress was tenuous. More critically, sacrificing basic psychological needs for autonomy, relatedness, and competence was robustly associated with ***reduced goal progress and increased psychological distress****. Thus, when people embark on the long and arduous road towards pursuing their long-term goals, it is critical that they do not sacrifice the basic psychological needs that will fuel them on this journey".* (St-Jacques, 2018)

Many studies have concluded that the sacrifice of basic psychological needs is counter-productive to your preparation process. Therefore, spare some time to satisfy these needs. You must interact with people be it your friends, family, or companion. You must spend time to relax and recuperate. This is of vital importance to your overall mental stability. There are a lot instances where officers have not exercised discretion and behaved in an emotionally incompetent way. This has got some relation to how they studied and the overall environment around them.

This doesn't mean that you must enjoy all the niceties of life while preparing for the exam.

When you decide to take this examination, it is understood that you might not be able to lead your *pre-aspirant* lives anymore. A certain amount of regulation and discipline is involved which includes changes in lifestyle, habits, and social circles. However, this doesn't entail social disconnectedness in its entirety and the aim is to avoid burnout at all costs.

Burnout happens when your body is so worked up that you cannot concentrate any longer. This will lead to disinterest, distress, and feeling of exhaustion and inefficiency. Therefore, manage your time and life in a way to avoid a burnout situation. Always remember what you are preparing for. The exam is just a test. You must prepare your body and mind for the larger struggle which is called life.

Balancing Preparation and Marriage

Marriage is a different ball game altogether. Once you are married you can no longer afford to be irresponsible. You have to take care of your family, provide for them, be their support and in turn prepare for the exam. So of vital importance in this regard is the support you get from your spouse. I was stupid enough not to discuss my next attempt with my wife. Don't make the same mistake. Therefore, set your priorities and communicate them to your spouse. This always involves giving and taking. Attend to their needs as well. Only a calm mind can prepare for the exam.

You must set targets and not overachieve them. Take time out for your family as and when you can. Discuss your topics with your spouse. Make the process interactive and engaging. Let them be a part of your overall journey. Most importantly, do not release your frustration on your family. They are your support system. You need to fully acknowledge this fact.

❑❑

Chapter 9

How to Stay Motivated?

The process of the UPSC Civil Service exam is physically and mentally draining. The constant ups and downs, peer pressure, financial problems, relationship issues, family pressure, etc., all add up to make this exam long and tough. So you must be motivated throughout the process. The primary sense of motivation is the very reason you begin the preparation. Secondary motivation comes from self-discipline. Some tips to stay motivated through self-discipline are discussed in this chapter:

1. The process is long and the syllabus is vast, therefore you must break it down. Make a timetable for the entire month or week and divide the syllabus accordingly. ***Set daily targets and achieve them***. This sense of achievement will give you satisfaction which will further propel you ahead. Don't jump from one portion of the syllabus to another. Rather, make a detailed study plan and stick to it. Everything takes time, in due course, you will be able to approach the syllabus systematically without much ado.

2. Cut the noise. Cut off all sources of distractions of any kind. ***For everyone, distractions are personal and there can be no generalization***. Some may learn from social media and some may spend hours doing nothing. It is your choice. Use your time on social media productively. Engage in channels and forums where actual learning or doubt clearing can happen.

3. Keep your social circle active and healthy. The fewer people you socialize with the less time wasted. ***Stay company with motivated individuals who share a common passion.*** Cut

off all relations which de-motivate you, drag you, and drain you. You need to keep your mind open and fresh. You cannot waste it on the kinds of stuff that add no value to your dream. You must be willing to sacrifice.

4. Eat healthily and stay hydrated. Long study hours, irregular eating habits, and stuffing junk food will only harm. Your health is very crucial. ***Only if you are healthy can you devote your energy***. Each day wasted in sickness will only cause regret therefore as it goes prevention is better than cure.

5. ***Exercise, play some sport, develop a hobby, meditate***. If you cannot spare time, then just get up and run for 20 minutes, it is enough to get you sweaty, lift your spirits and bring fresh thoughts. These days so many online skilling courses are there, you can even learn some different courses just to gain knowledge and bring some change to your daily schedule.

6. ***Learn something new each day***. It can be anything and not necessarily belong to your syllabus. But anything which brings freshness to your daily life.

7. If you have already given more than two years, I would suggest upgrading your skills and seeking employment first. ***A busy mind is better than an idle mind***. Financial freedom is very important and I have already stated enough about that in previous chapters.

8. Take time to rest and recuperate. ***Fix a day in a week or in a fortnight where you can relax and enjoy your time***. Go out and have fun. Watch movies or your favourite web series. Cooling off is a must otherwise, fatigue will set in and it will affect your learning process.

9. Listen to struggle stories. Listen to the journey of those who have made it. Learn from their mistakes. ***Listen to everyone but follow only the path which suits you best***.

10. Whenever you feel dejected, just get up, do some work out or cardio, or play some sport.

There is a beautiful line in Shawshank Redemption- ***"All it takes is time and pressure"***. Persistence is the key. Failure will come but so will success. You must not get depressed about any bad scores during the mock test. It's good that you failed in practice. You now know what you don't have to do in the actual test. So every failure is a learning experience.

Train your mind to only seek positives. Enjoy the journey. One day all that struggle will be worth it. One day all parties lost, all gatherings unattended, and all wedding invites declined will be worth it. So enjoy the process. You are in the process of entering the Steel Frame of the country, so take pride and continuously march ahead.

Key Takeaways

This part was intended to answer some of the most basic queries of the aspirants. There are several myths surrounding these queries which often demotivate the aspirants. Further, a lot of time, energy, and money are wasted if due diligence is not practised in deciding the course of study. Most importantly, this part was intended to make you feel that you can prepare for this exam from anywhere in this world.

It was also focused on balancing your life. Becoming emotionally and mentally more competent. It's a myth that one cannot prepare for this exam while working or while in a marriage.

Certainly, it is tough but not impossible. And what good is a challenge if it's not tough?

It is just an exam that requires a systematic approach. But in doing that you must keep your motivation level high and stay healthy. The last part of this book is intended to dive deep into the issue of joblessness among the aspirants, the *"aspirant syndrome"*, how to overcome failure, and how to get going despite multiple setbacks.

❑❑

PART III

Civil Services and Beyond

Organized Civil Services in India have their origin in the British Raj. However, a rudimentary form of civil services is found in pre-British history as well. Many designations of officers are mentioned in numerous historical records. Even during the Mauryan Age, some form of civil services and competitive exams are mentioned in the Arthashastra. Therefore, Civil Services in India have a long history, and therefore no wonder that the charm of Civil Services continues to this day.

The craze for Civil Services has not diminished even after the LPG reforms of 1991 whereby the private sector exploded to an unprecedented level.

This trend begs a question, why do Civil Services continue to garner such attention, and is it worth it? The answer to the first question I have answered in the first part of this book. The last part of this book will explore the answer to the second question.

This part will also focus on the larger problem of joblessness and how this hysterical craze for civil services is accentuating this problem. Part of the reason lies in romanticizing the services making them larger than life. The hangover of the *'Heaven Born'* service of the English Sahib has not disappeared in its entirety. We continue to marvel at the power and perks of the bureaucrats and in return are more and more attracted to it. This attraction inevitably leads to the government sector and creates an illusion that a government job is considered the safest.

In the pursuit of this safe and powerful career, lakhs of youth squander their precious time in preparation. Most of them do not even realize why they are preparing. And yet many don't even realize when they should have stopped and introspected. It is a fact that as a country develops the role of bureaucracy diminishes or changes more towards facilitation. However, it is weird that in our country, even after passing with meritorious degrees like

B.Tech, MBA, MBBS, etc. people opt for the Civil Services and when they fail many settle for SSC, Bank PO, etc.

This part is also for those who have failed repeatedly and do not find the way out. I can understand their frustration and sense of helplessness. What are the things you need to do and how can you change your approach? All these will be discussed in this part. This part is not sugarcoated and is not meant to please or motivate you. It is aimed to jolt you and awaken you to reality.

❑❑

Chapter

10

The Aspirant Syndrome

You started the preparation and were confident that you will clear the exam. Your friends were confident and so was your family. You gave your everything to the exam, day in and day out. The results are announced and forget about interviews, you couldn't even clear the prelims. You are shocked and devastated. But you didn't lose hope. You prepare again, this time you sacrificed it all and just focused on the study.

But again, you don't clear. The cycle begins next time because now you are struck by the UPSC bug.

You cannot come out. You have already devoted two years, how can you lose hope? You study again with less motivation, you don't fare well, you lie to your family, you are unemployed, you now live only to clear the prelims. But you fail again. The cycle repeats itself and each time you are less motivated and more frustrated. Finally, your attempts are over and so is your youth.

This is the dark side of the Civil Service Exam. You just keep repeating the same mistakes again and again. You are never really sure what went wrong. By the time, the mark sheet is out, you have already filled the form for next year and decided on the optional without even knowing what went wrong. This is true for 90 percent of the candidate who appears for the exam.

The pain of individual failure is deadened by the antidote of blaming everyone, even the government. So in the process, you are writing the answers while being critical of the government and its policies. This is not what is intended. This contradiction becomes more and more apparent as time goes by. Lastly, the aspirant turns into an activist which is reflected in the answers. Gradually, the aspirant starts to enjoy his or her stay in Delhi. He/she is content in debating with her peers. The knowledge showoff in local discussions becomes more important. The sense of aura which is attributed to such aspirants by newcomers provides solace from the apparent failure in the exam.

This is the ***"aspirant syndrome".*** They are so comfortable being an aspirant that they have forgotten why they started the preparation. The transformation of an aspirant into an activist is the last nail. The negativity and criticism of the system take complete control of your thought process. You turn out to be more depressed and more frustrated. So why wait till this eventuality?

There is an obsession with social media these days and the first category which I want to discuss is with reference to social media often you get so immersed in social media content that you will end up following every topper available on the platform, their every post, activity. Whenever, you find yourself falling into this bottomless pit of scrolling, stop and ask yourself is this really worth your time? My advice to you will be to avoid wasting your time on things which won't be fruitful in the preparation journey. Instead use that time in exploring the content that is relevant for your syllabus.

Then you have got some aspirants who have become more of an activist. They prefer to indulge in debates, discussions and discouraging others around them. They have the knowledge but they are applying it somewhere they shouldn't. They will purchase every new book in the shop just to show off. While some aspirants are not even clear about what they want in life. They are so easily manipulated, that their strategy changes as soon as they talk to the next person.

Yet another category of aspirants is daydreamers. You can site them in groups, talking and fantasizing about LBSNAA. Some have come to Delhi not to prepare but to find a suitable mate. Are you falling in any one of these categories? If yes, then I sincerely advise you not to waste your time and pursue some other career. These categories are a classic example of the "aspirant syndrome". But if you do not fall into any of the above categories, you are in for the serious competition. As I said earlier, your competition is not with 5-6 lakh candidates who appear for the exam. Your competition is with those few thousands who slog day and night to chase their dream.

Take Control of Your Life

Failure is a stepping stone only for some time. After which it becomes a wake-up call. Two successive failed attempts should be enough to wake you up. As I stated in earlier chapters, one and a half years of dedicated preparation is sufficient to build a strong foundation. The rest is application. So after two failed attempts, you are not lacking in knowledge. You are lacking in its application and for that, you need not give 100 percent of your time to studying. The application requires 4-5 hours of dedicated study which can be done with the job. So it is highly recommended that you seek employment. Gain practical real-world experience. This will boost your confidence and morale. You are no longer dependent on anyone and so you can now direct the course of your study.

It is beneficial for your overall growth if you keep your skills at par with the latest developments. Never lose touch with your graduation subjects. Always upgrade your skills as per the demand of the market. Believe me, whatever you do, you will end up in excel sheets. So take new courses as and when you can.

Nowadays so many apps and courses are available online to keep abreast with the latest developments around you. Many aspirants join some NGOs or such non-profit association which provide hands-on experience of real-world problems. It is a good opportunity to gain some remuneration and also acquire practical experience. You may also develop your podcast, and video tutorials for YouTube and gain remuneration as content development. Or you can teach or evaluate answers in any coaching institute.

But whatever you do be financially independent after two successive failed attempts. Take control of your life and don't be dependent on anyone. This will relieve you of so much stress and the peace of mind you gain will help you to focus more on your studies.

Know When to Stop

I cleared the 2015 Civil Services Exam and joined IRS in 2016. But, even after that, I wanted to clear this exam to become an IAS officer. I gave a few more attempts but each with less motivation. I quietly started to enjoy my work as Assistant Commissioner and I gradually realized I was appearing for the exam only to satisfy my inflated ego.

Once I even fought with my wife saying "I have to clear the UPSC so I will appear for this exam", it's her reply that ended my reverie. She said,

"Haven't you cleared it already, what else do you want to prove?". It was only then I stopped my futile attempts. So is it the case with you as well? If you are already selected, please ask yourself why are you still making further attempts? For yourself or your ego? Always be true to yourself. You may be giving all sorts of reasons to everyone but deep down you must be able to convince yourself.

There are many examples where aspirants have left the preparation at the right time and pursued a successful career elsewhere. You must understand that the Civil Services are not everything. There is an inverse relationship between the level of development of a country and the attraction towards the Civil Services. As the country progresses, the private sector takes most of the roles of government in providing quality service to the people. Today our country is at a cusp of a revolution. Even the high-ranking profile of Deputy Secretary/Joint Secretary is now open for lateral entry. Though it may have its merit and demerit, the point is, that the government is gradually opening up for the private sector across the world.

Today, everybody is looking for skills. Whether it is the private or government sector.

Apply Your Knowledge

Having said that now I will explain what application of knowledge means. You have studied hard. We all do. You don't lack knowledge. Everybody knows what to study. The way ahead is practice and revision. Revision is as neglected in the preparation as the leg is neglected in the workout. Your retention will decrease if your revision is not proper. Dedicate a day in a week only for revision. This is a must and should not be neglected at any cost.

Further, you need to practice. And here comes the importance of test series. Enrol in any test series you want but your aim should be to practise at least 5,000 questions before prelims. A plethora of tests is available online free of cost. Many aspirants don't appear for the tests for the simple fear of not wanting to face their failure. This strategy may work for some but for the rest, it is doomed to fail.

Another important reason for not appearing for the tests is that you feel you are not ready. You haven't studied the full syllabus. Believe me, you will never be able to finish the entire syllabus. So stop giving excuses and face the tests. You have to be truthful to yourself. Only you can judge your performance and only you know your level. So if you are shying away from the tests, know that you are keeping yourself in the dark. And nothing can be more dangerous.

Another important aspect of mock tests is that it shows you where you stand in the all India competition. It will give you an overall perspective of your preparation and you can then improve accordingly. Attempt the tests and evaluate your score each time. Learn what you didn't know and revise what you learned before. Keep repeating this. And this is true even for mains.

The more you practise the more you learn. The importance of tests cannot be emphasized enough. Even if you have not studied everything, still attempt the tests and repeat the cycle above. You will see a marked improvement in your scores. The mock test allows you to strategize for the actual exam.

Take full advantage of it. Don't be scared or depressed that you didn't perform well. It is fine. Learn from your mistakes and improve upon them. That's the entire purpose of the test series. So just attempt as many tests as possible. The more you sweat in practice the less you bleed in war and UPSC is a war.

❑❑

Chapter

11

What is a Failure?

You are measuring failure in binary terms. If you cleared the exam you are successful and if you don't you are a failure. You are not alone in subscribing to this notion. We have all done this at some point in our life. This is fundamentally wrong. Firstly, no one can determine the success or failure of a person in terms of one exam. Secondly, by subscribing to this notion, you will be doing more harm to yourself.

The preparation for the UPSC Civil Services exam is hard. It takes a toll on your life. Precious years of youth are wasted in pursuing a dream. You invest so much time in this exam that you cut yourself from society and from the skills you have acquired in your academic course. If you are successful, you enter the corridors of power, otherwise you are left with few options. So clearly this is not the intention of this exam, and this is not how the exam should have been attempted.

On top of that, many institutes have started campaigns like "clear prelims in the first attempt", "clear the UPSC in 100 days", etc. Success stories of toppers are also presented in a way as if it is a cakewalk. This is disturbing. Many aspirants work tirelessly for years, and such campaigns serve only to demean their hard work. As I stated in earlier chapters, don't believe in such campaigns. Only believe in your struggle and your story. Never demean yourself just because you have failed. You may have failed one exam, that doesn't define your life. ***Life is bigger than the sum total of all your personal and shared experiences***.

Take a Break and Introspect

Repeated failure in the exam requires serious introspection. If you keep attempting the exam without analysing your mistake, you will repeat the same mistakes over and over. You cannot expect change unless you change your approach. Take a break, for a year if need be. But, turn away from your studies for a while, and analyse your mistakes. If your option is tough for you then change it.

Many aspirants are scared of changing their options. They make the excuse that they have already invested time, money, and energy then why change it at this juncture. This is the classic "sunk-cost fallacy". Your time, money, and energy is already gone, so don't bother about it. Think of the future. Just because you have invested in a bad project doesn't mean you have to continue.

Don't bother whether the subject you have chosen is favoured or not. There is no such thing, all it takes is your interest and your ability to answer the questions, that's it. Therefore, to change the approach, think differently and try new options. This will give you a much-needed fresh breath in your study. Don't be afraid to embrace the change.

Open Up

Get in touch with your friends and family. Share your feelings with your closest confidantes. Relieve your stress. Take that much-needed holiday if you want. But take a break. Generally, aspirants don't share their feelings. Since in the process of preparation you have dissociated yourself from so many people it is important to get back to society. Don't keep all your stress to yourself.

If you have failed, so have nearly 95 percent of those who applied. You are not alone. Share your emotions on forums that provide for anonymity. Talk, don't isolate yourself. Your family understands you. Your friends understand you. Nothing is more important than your life. And you are most important to your family. At the end of the day, the Civil Service Exam is just another exam, so take it like that.

Your chance of clearing this exam depends on so many factors that no one can guarantee whether you will make it or not. Also, don't feel ashamed that people are clearing the exam in 100 days of study. It is not like that. Let the competition be healthy and don't add hysteria to it. You have studied and that's all that matters. Don't fall for these advertisements and don't glamourize or celebrate UPSC toppers. They are just aspirants who cleared. Nothing more nothing less. You are not below anyone.

So open up and talk. Don't let the pressure inside you overcome all aspects of your being. Study hard but keep the competition humane. Not everything is UPSC, people are far more successful elsewhere too, and contribute to nation building. And always remember you are not alone.

Keep the Exam Simple

As I mentioned in the introduction of this part, the craze for the Civil Service exam is getting more pronounced with each passing day. What it results in is of critical importance to the overall growth and development of this country. Of all the aspirants who appear for this exam, roughly 1,000 odd candidates make it into the bureaucracy. Half a million or so candidates will repeat the exam. Of the 1,000 odd candidates, nearly 80 percent will again appear for the exam in pursuit of better service or a better cadre. So roughly every year only 200-300 candidates are the ones who do not appear again.

Since the career in the Civil Service inspires so much admiration, aspirants pursue it for an average of 4 to 5 years. This is not healthy. The longer you pursue the exam, the more you are cut off from your basic graduation subject. These days, due to technological changes, skills are coming up and getting outdated on a day-to-day basis. So by investing a critical amount of time, you spend your youth not in upgrading any useful skill but only in pursuit of an exam. It is no wonder that quality education is not matching the desired employability. The same skills which could have been used in a proper way are now wasted.

After two years of repeated failure, you must not waste any more time and gain employment. Your core skill set must not be lost. At the same time, you must be market relevant so learn new skills and be up to date. A serious preparation of one and a half years is sufficient to build the foundation. Therefore, focus more on practice. At last, keep this exam as simple and as humane as you can.

❑❑

Conclusion

The book essentially aims to focus on the why, how and what of the UPSC Civil Exam Preparation. It urges you to be very clear as to why you want to join the Civil Services. Your motivation will not only decide your future but also the quality of your personal and professional life. Moreover, it provides a comparison between corporate jobs and Civil Services with their own set of pros and cons. You must decide what you want after due diligence.

Part 1 of the book also explores the importance of job satisfaction in the bureaucracy and beyond money what makes the Civil Services special.

Part II of the book explores "How" to actually prepare for the exam. It outlines the pros and cons of coaching vs self-study and also provides options of preparing for the exam from the comfort of the home. It also busts several myths associated with the exam to provide a clear picture to the aspirants.

Part III of the book focuses on failure and life beyond the Civil Services. One must not simply waste our precious years in mindless pursuit of a dream. Whatever decision you make must be after due scrutiny. The very definition of failure is contested. Failure is not what everyone else thinks. You decide your own failure. But whatever you do, don't lose out on critical skill sets which will help you forever in life. Today, you need to be marketable whether it is the civil service or private sector.

I have endeavoured to provide as many aspects to the preparation as possible. I have not dealt with the usual preparation steps and guidelines because you all know it. As I said, ***this is Not Your Usual UPSC Book***.

❑❑

References

Demmke, C. (2019). *Legitimacy of Civil Services* in the 21st Century.

Epstein, D. (2019). *Range : Why Generalists Triumph in a Specialized World.*

Grievances, D. O. (2010). *Civil Services Survey.*

Indian Institute of Management. (2015). A Study of Comparing Salaries/Emoluments in the Government Sector vis-à-vis CPSU/Private Sector in India. 321.

Indian Institute of Management. (n.d.). A Study of Comparing S.

Klein, D. K. (2009). Condition for Intuitive Expertise : A Failure to Disagree.

Ryan and Deci. (2017).

🕮 References 🕮

St-Jacques, A. (2018). *Sacrificial Goals: The Antecedents and Consequences of Sacrificing Basic Psychological Needs.* McGill University, Montreal, QC, Canada.

❑❑